JAPANESE

COOKING

FOR TWO

JAPANESE

COOKING

FOR TWO

Simple to make,
authentic Japanese dishes

Kurumi Hayter

CHARTWELL
BOOKS, INC.

To my husband Simon,
for his support and encouragement.
And with special thanks to my mother Keiko.

A QUINTET BOOK

Published by Chartwell Books
A Division of Book Sales, Inc.
114 Northfield Avenue
Edison, New Jersey 08837

This edition produced for sale in the U.S.A., its
territories and dependencies only.

ISBN 0-7858-0632-6

This book was designed and produced by
Quintet Publishing Limited
6 Blundell Street
London N7 9BH

CREATIVE DIRECTOR: *Richard Dewing*
DESIGNER: *Simon Balley*
PROJECT EDITOR: *Diana Steedman*
EDITOR: *Deborah Taylor*
PHOTOGRAPHER: *David Armstrong*

Typeset in Great Britain by
Central Southern Typesetters, Eastbourne
Manufactured by Eray Scan Pte Ltd, Singapore
Printed by Star Standard Industries (Pte) Ltd, Singapore

ACKNOWLEDGMENTS

The Publishers are grateful to Také Ltd,
Camden Town, London, to
Asuka Japanese Restaurant, Baker Street, London,
and to Mrs Yuko Hishitani for supplying
crockery for photography.

CONTENTS

PREFACE

The cuisine of Southeast Asia has enjoyed a boom in popularity over the past few years, and it is now common to find books on Thai and Indonesian cooking (to name but two) on the shelves of most book stores. So it is surprising that many people find themselves hard put to name any Japanese foods, with the exception of the most famous dishes like Tempura and Sushi, when asked what Japanese foods they are familiar with. People invariably think of Japanese cooking and its preparation as an esoteric art requiring years of training and experience to master. This misunderstanding is a great pity, because Japanese cooking not only encompasses as great a variety of flavors and textures as any other country in Asia, but also, for the most part, is easily and quickly prepared.

This book aims to introduce a wide selection of delicious recipes that require no special skills or training to prepare. I sincerely hope that both the eating and making of the dishes in this book are a pleasurable and interesting experience.

INTRODUCTION

THE FLAVORS OF JAPANESE CUISINE

The three basic flavors of cooking are saltiness, sweetness, and sourness. These flavors are produced in Japanese cooking by the use, either singly or in combination, of the following "building block" ingredients:

- soy sauce
- *miso* (a fermented soybean paste)
- Japanese rice wine or *sake*
- *mirin* (a mixture of a variant of *sake* with sugar)
- *dashi* (a Japanese stock made from dried bonito or dried kelp or a mixture of the two, depending on the flavor desired)
- sea salt

- sugar (preferably superfine)

BASIC TECHNIQUES

One of the great advantages to Japanese cooking is that to begin experimenting requires little investment in equipment over and above what is contained in the average Western kitchen. As for ingredients, the purchase of a bottle of Japanese soy sauce, *sake, mirin*, and some instant *dashi* granules (the latter two are widely available from health-food stores or Japanese or Chinese food departments) will enable any cook to prepare most of the recipes in this book.

Broadly speaking, there are three methods of preparation commonly used by the Japanese cook.

Broiling or *YAKI-MONO*

Broiling is the fastest cooking technique in the Japanese repertoire. Most commonly the meat, fish or vegetable prepared in this manner is first skewered before being cooked. In many cases, broiling takes place after the food has been steeped in a marinade. Sometimes it is brushed with a sauce or glaze while being broiled. A technique used when cooking fish involves the liberal sprinkling of salt onto the fish prior to broiling.

Simmering or *NI-MONO*

Ni-mono dishes commonly feature a mixture of either meat and vegetables or fish and vegetables and, less often, just fish or vegetables on their own. Some *ni-mono* require the use of a stock, whereas others depend only on the inclusion of soy sauce, *mirin,* and occasionally sugar or *sake* to enhance their flavor.

Deep frying or *AGE-MONO*

Tempura, possibly the most widely known ambassador of Japanese cooking, is only one of a number of deep-fried dishes in the Japanese repertoire, which includes deep-fried vegetables, fish, and meats. A number of different coatings are used in Japanese deep frying, including a batter of all-purpose flour in the case of *Tempura,* potato flour, and bread crumbs.

PREPARING MEAT

Very thinly sliced meat is common in Japanese cooking. An advantage of thin slicing is that it creates an impression of volume even with small amounts. Also, thin slices cook quickly. If you cannot find thinly sliced meat, ask a butcher to slice it or half-freeze the piece of meat you purchase and then slice it yourself.

PREPARING VEGETABLES

There are three cutting styles used by Japanese cooks.

1 *Ran giri*, or chopping at random. Peel, then roll around in your hand each time you chop, cutting to create asymmetrical shapes.

2 *Naname wa-giri*, or slicing on a slant. Cut on a slant to create larger pieces.

3 *Sengiri*, or slicing into matchsticks. Cut larger slices into matchstick-sized pieces.

THE ETIQUETTE OF EATING

Chopsticks, one of many Chinese inventions that have been assimilated into Japanese culture, are called *o-hashi*. Using chopsticks is no more difficult than using a knife and fork, as long as the user knows the correct way to hold them. Follow the directions illustrated below, and you should have no problem eating with *o-hashi*.

❶ Think of your chopsticks as jaws that have been turned upside down. The lower chopstick, clamped between the tip of your ring finger, inner joint of your thumb, and the knuckle of your index finger, remains fixed in the same position during eating.

❷ The upper chopstick is then held in the tips of your middle and index fingers and thumb so that it can be opened and closed in relation to the lower chopstick.

There are some basic principles of etiquette:

- Don't hold your chopsticks over a dish while deciding what to eat (*mayoi-bashi*).
- Don't spear food with your chopsticks (*sashi-bashi*).
- Don't use your chopsticks to pull a dish toward you or push it away from you (*yose-bashi*).
- Never pass food between chopsticks, as this mirrors the Buddhist practice of handling the bones of the dead (*hashi-watashi*).
- Use your left hand to hold the rice bowl and your right hand to use your chopsticks. For left-handers, the reverse is correct.
- In a formal situation, do not eat food directly from a large, communal dish. Instead, first place food from the large dish into the small dish that is provided for your individual portion and then eat from that.
- Japanese noodles, or *men*, can be slurped with gusto while holding the noodles between your chopsticks. But Japanese soups or *sui-mono* should be sipped with more reserve.

PREPARING AND SERVING A JAPANESE MEAL

The Western concept of serving a dinner as a succession of courses is alien to traditional Japanese cooking. All the dishes in a Japanese meal are served to the diner as a set, with the exception of dessert, which is not considered an integral part of a Japanese meal, although fresh fruits are often provided at the end together with green tea. A true Japanese dinner always includes rice, a soup, and a small dish of Japanese pickles, which are accompanied by a main dish of fish or meat together with a small side dish. A larger arrangement, for example at a dinner party, would be achieved by adding a second side dish and perhaps a second main dish as well, depending on the occasion. A good host will attempt to vary each of the dishes so that the meal will combine as many different flavors, textures, and types of preparation as possible. An example of this food-combining for a dinner party might be: broiled fish and deep fried chicken nuggets served as main dishes, braised soybeans and spinach sprinkled with sesame seeds and soy sauce as side dishes, and rice, a soup, and a small serving of pickled vegetables as accompaniments. You may wonder how the cook manages to juggle so many dishes simultaneously and serve them all at once. The simple answer is that generally Japanese cooks make most of the dishes well in advance. Some dishes are re-heated prior to serving; others are served warm rather than hot. Exceptions to this include dishes cooked at the table such as *sukiyaki*, soups and noodles which should always be fresh and hot.

Japanese drinks

Today, the traditional Japanese rice liquor, *sake*, is a less frequent accompaniment to a Japanese dinner than it used to be. Many Japanese now choose lager-type beers to drink at their dinner table.

JAPANESE FISH STOCK

D A S H I

Dashi or Japanese Fish Stock, is an essential ingredient in Japanese cooking. It can be made from *katsuo-bushi* (flaked bonito) or *konbu* (kelp). Some *dashi* is a combination of the two variants, and it is this version that is given here. There are two classes of *dashi*: "premier," which is used in Japanese bouillion, *chawan mushi*, and *miso* soup, and normal *dashi*, which is suitable for simmered dishes and noodles or for use as a supplement to premier *dashi*.

PREMIER DASHI	NORMAL DASHI
MAKES ABOUT 4 CUPS STOCK	**MAKES 4 CUPS STOCK**
4 cups water	*4¼ cups water*
6 in strip dried konbu or kelp, cut into three pieces	*dried konbu and bonito flakes from making Premier dashi*
1 oz dried bonito flakes	*½ oz dried bonito flakes*

❶ Put the water and *konbu* in a pan and slowly bring to a boil over a medium heat. Just before the liquid reaches boiling point, remove the *konbu* and add the *bonito* flakes. When the flakes begin to rise and the liquid bubbles, turn off the heat. Wait until the flakes have sunk to the bottom of the pan.

❶ Put the water, used *konbu* and *bonito* flakes, and the dried *bonito* flakes in a pan together. Bring to a boil and simmer over medium heat until the liquid has reduced by about a third. Strain through cheesecloth or a large coffee filter.

❷ The *konbu* and *bonito* flakes can be retained to make normal *dashi* at another time.

DASHI STOCK GRANULES
Instant dashi can be made from freeze-dried bouillion granules, which is a convenient, no-fuss alternative, although opinions differ as to whether the taste of instant dashi is a match for the "real thing" or not. If you buy instant dashi and the instructions turn out to be in Japanese, use the following instructions.

In a pan, stir 1 heaped teaspoon of granules into 1¼ cups of cold water and bring to a boil.

MISO SOUP with Wakame Seaweed and Onion

WAKAME TO TAMA-NEGI NO MISO-SHIRU

Miso shiru is the easiest soup you will ever make. In Japan, it is served at breakfast, lunch or dinner, when it is accompanied by a main dish and a bowl of rice.

Wakame seaweed and tofu are the two most common ingredients used in the soup and are either used alone or are complemented by fresh chopped vegetables. Miso soup varies according to the tastes of every family, and each household has its own favorite combinations.

Unlike Western soups, Japanese soup is sipped from the bowl, with any pieces of vegetable or tofu being eaten with chopsticks.

INGREDIENTS

2 cups dashi stock (see p. 13)
½ medium onion, sliced
2 teaspoons dried wakame seaweed
2 tablespoons miso paste

1 Put the dashi stock and onion in a pan, bring to a boil, and simmer until the onion becomes transparent.

2 Add the wakame and continue to simmer until it has expanded. (This only takes a couple of minutes.)

3 Add the miso paste and stir, using a small egg beater, until dissolved. Heat for a few more minutes until the soup starts to boil. Do not boil for more than 1–2 minutes or the soup will be too salty. Serve immediately.

MISO SOUP with Silken *Tofu* and Scallions

KINU DOFU TO NEGI NO MISO-SHIRU

Two types of *tofu* are widely used in Japanese cooking, *kinu* or silken *tofu* and *momen* or cotton *tofu*. As the names suggest, *kinu dofu* has a very smooth, silky texture, whereas *momen dofu* is characterized by its more solid, coarser appearance and feel. It is *kinu dofu* that is usually used in *miso* soups.

INGREDIENTS

2 cups dashi stock (see p. 13)
4 oz silken tofu, cut into ½ in cubes
3 scallions, chopped
2 tablespoons miso paste

1 Put the *dashi* stock and *tofu* in a pan, bring to a boil, and simmer for 4–5 minutes.

2 Add the scallions and simmer for a further minute. Stir the *miso* paste into the soup using a mini egg beater until it is completely dissolved. Simmer again until the soup just returns to a boil. Serve immediately.

EGG AND LEEK Bouillion

TAMAGO NO SUMASHI JIRU

This clear soup is usually eaten with *sushi* dishes and has a subtle flavor. The use of shiitake mushrooms adds extra taste. Do not boil the leek for too long as it needs to retain some of its texture.

INGREDIENTS

2 cups dashi stock (see p. 13)
1 in leek, halved and sliced very finely
3 shiitake mushrooms, sliced
½ teaspoon salt
A dash of soy sauce
1 egg, beaten

❶ In a pan bring the *dashi* stock to a boil, then add the leek, mushrooms, salt, and soy sauce. Simmer for 3–4 minutes.

❷ Gradually add the beaten egg to the pan, beating continuously to stop it from forming lumps. Serve immediately.

SIMMERED BEEF and Potatoes

GYUNIKU NO NIKU-JAGA

This dish is one of several described in Japan as "mother's taste dishes," and it is very much a family-style creation.

INGREDIENTS

¼ cup water

1½ tablespoons sake

2 tablespoons sugar

2 tablespoons soy sauce

½ lb thinly sliced beef, cut into 2 in lengths

½ lb potatoes, peeled and cut into bite-sized pieces

½ cup frozen peas

1 Put the water, *sake*, sugar, and soy sauce in a pan and bring to a boil.

2 Add the meat and simmer for a few minutes or until the meat browns. Remove from the pan and set aside. Put the potatoes in the pan and simmer, covered, for 10 minutes or until tender. Add the peas and simmer for a further 3 minutes.

3 Return the meat to the pan and simmer for about 3 minutes. Serve hot with a bowl of rice and one or two vegetable dishes.

HAMBURGERS with Shiitake Mushroom Sauce

BEEF HAMBURGER NO SHIITAKE SAUSU

This is a contemporary combination of Western substance with Japanese form. The sauce retains the delicate flavor of the shiitake mushrooms partnered by the punchy flavors of the ginger and soy sauce.

INGREDIENTS
⅓ cup vegetable oil
1 small onion, finely chopped
8 slices wholewheat bread made into bread crumbs
1½ tablespoons milk
½ lb ground beef
½ teaspoon salt
Freshly ground black pepper
½ egg, beaten

FOR THE SHIITAKE SAUCE
2 oz shiitake mushrooms, sliced
¼ cup water
1 tablespoon sake
1 tablespoon soy sauce
½ in piece gingerroot, peeled
2 teaspoons cornstarch

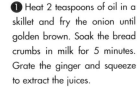

❶ Heat 2 teaspoons of oil in a skillet and fry the onion until golden brown. Soak the bread crumbs in milk for 5 minutes. Grate the ginger and squeeze to extract the juices.

❷ Place the beef, onion, seasoning, and egg in a bowl and mix thoroughly.

❸ Divide the mixture into two. Moisten your hands with water, then shape into burgers.

❹ Heat the remaining oil in the skillet and saute the burgers for about 5 minutes on each side or until cooked. Remove and set aside.

❺ Add the shiitake mushrooms to the skillet, then add the water, *sake*, soy sauce, and ginger juice. Season with salt and pepper. Bring to a boil and cook for 1 minute before adding the cornstarch diluted in a small amount of water, to thicken. Pour over the burgers and serve.

STEAK with Garlic and Soy Sauce

STEAK NO NIN-NIKU SAUSU

A combination of a Western cut of meat with a Japanese sauce that works really well. Remember that the cooking times given for the steak will vary depending on the thickness of the meat and personal preference. This flexible dish can be served with Japanese side dishes or a Western accompaniment of vegetables.

INGREDIENTS

2 x 4–8 oz sirloin or rump steaks
Freshly ground black pepper
1 tablespoon vegetable oil
5 garlic cloves, sliced
1 tablespoon sake
2 tablespoons butter
1 tablespoon soy sauce

1 Beat the meat on both sides using a steak hammer or a rolling pin, then season with the pepper.

2 Heat the oil in a skillet and saute the garlic briefly. Remove and set aside.

3 Saute the steaks lightly on both sides, then add the *sake* and cook for a further minute before placing the steaks on warmed serving plates.

4 Return the garlic to the pan, add the butter and soy sauce, and when the mixture begins to bubble, pour it over the steaks and serve immediately.

SUGGESTED COOKING TIMES
(For 4–8 oz steak)

Rare: 3 minutes on each side
Medium-rare: 4 minutes on each side Well-done: 6 minutes on each side

STIR-FRIED PORK in Ginger with Onion

BUTA-NIKU NO SHOUGA YAKI

he sweet, tangy flavors of the soy sauce and ginger marinade are enriched and enhanced by the pork. Like most other Japanese dishes, *Buta-niku no shouga yaki* is easy to prepare and can be made in no time at all.

INGREDIENTS

½ lb thinly sliced pork, cut into 2 in lengths

1 tablespoon vegetable oil

1 medium onion, peeled and sliced

FOR THE MARINADE

1 oz gingerroot , peeled, grated, and squeezed

1½ tablespoons soy sauce

1 tablespoon sake

1 To make the marinade, mix together the juice of the ginger, the soy sauce, and the *sake* in a bowl.

2 Add the pork and marinate for 30 minutes. Heat the oil in a skillet and saute the onion until it is transparent. Remove and set aside.

3 Add the meat to the skillet and saute for 5 minutes or until cooked.

4 Return the onion to the skillet and stir-fry for a further 1–2 minutes.

5 Add the remaining marinade and stir-fry again for 1–2 minutes. Serve with a bowl of hot, plain boiled rice.

SIMMERED PORK and Mouli

DAIKON TO BARA-NIKU NO UMA-NI

Simmering is a widely used technique in Japanese cooking, as it brings out the flavors of the ingredients. The western equivalent of the Japanese giant radish, or *daikon*, the mouli, contains more water, making it easier to cook. Taste-wise though, there is little difference between the two.

INGREDIENTS

2 teaspoons vegetable oil
½ lb pork, cut into ½ in lengths
½ lb mouli, peeled and chopped into randomly shaped, bite-sized pieces
3 tablespoons sake
2 tablespoons soy sauce

1 Heat the oil in a saucepan and add the meat. Saute until browned.

2 Add the mouli and stir well, then add the *sake* and simmer, covered, for 10 minutes.

3 Add the soy sauce and continue to cook, covered, for a further 5 minutes or until the mouli is cooked through. Serve hot with a bowl of boiled rice.

DEEP-FRIED PORK Steak in Bread Crumbs

TONKATSU

This is one of the most popular dishes in modern Japanese cuisine. It is usually served with shredded cabbage and garnished with tomato ketchup, brown sauce, and/or mustard.

INGREDIENTS

2 x 4–8 oz boneless pork loin steaks
2 tablespoons all-purpose flour
1 egg, beaten
2–3 tablespoons dry white bread crumbs
Vegetable oil, for deep frying

1 Beat the meat gently with a steak hammer or rolling pin to tenderize it. Dust with the flour, then dip into the beaten egg.

2 Coat the steaks with the bread crumbs.

3 Heat the oil to 330°F and then deep-fry the steaks until cooked through, about 6 minutes, depending on the thickness of the steaks. Serve garnished with lettuce, sliced tomato and cucumber, adding tomato ketchup, brown sauce, and mustard if you wish.

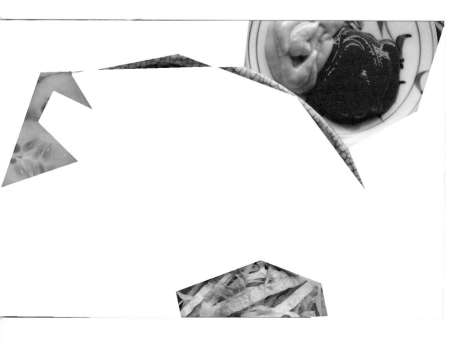

PORK MEATBALLS in Sweet Soy Sauce

NIKU-DANGO NO AMAKARA-NI

The use of minced meat is widespread in Japan, and this form, *niku-dango*, is sold ready-made in delicatessens as well as being prepared at home. Take care, as the sweet-tasting sauce makes it all too easy to gorge on these little balls of pork!

MAKES 16 MEATBALLS

FOR THE MEATBALLS

½ lb ground pork
¼ cup finely chopped leek
1 tablespoon sake
A large pinch of salt
½ egg, beaten
1 tablespoon cornstarch
Vegetable oil, for deep frying

FOR THE SAUCE

4 tablespoons water
1 tablespoon sake
1 tablespoon mirin
1 tablespoon sugar
1 tablespoon soy sauce
2 teaspoons cornstarch

1 To make the meatballs, mix the pork, leek, *sake*, salt, beaten egg, and cornstarch in a bowl. Knead the mixture until the beaten egg is well combined and gives a stickiness to the rest of the mixture. Then, take one tablespoon of the mixture in your hand and mold it into a ball.

2 Fill a pan about one-third full with cooking oil. Heat to 350°F and then deep-fry the meatballs for 5 minutes or until browned. Remove and drain off any excess oil on paper towels.

3 Put the water, s*ake*, *mirin*, sugar, soy sauce, and cornstarch together in a pan. Mix together over low heat, stirring until the sauce has thickened. Add the meatballs and continue to stir until they are all covered in the sauce. Serve with a bowl of hot, plain boiled rice and a vegetable dish.

JAPANESE CHICKEN Shish Kebab

YAKITORI

Yakitori lends its name to the Japanese *yakitori* bar, a popular place to meet, eat, drink, and socialize throughout Japan. Chicken and chicken livers are the two most commonly eaten *yakitori*. They can be eaten with a sweet, soy sauce-based sauce or *tare*, as in the recipe below, or sprinkled liberally with salt or powdered chili.

INGREDIENTS

FOR THE SAUCE	FOR THE YAKITORI
¼ cup soy sauce	2 boneless chicken breasts (with skin) diced, making 24 pieces
¼ cup mirin	
1 tablespoon sugar	1 leek, cut into 1 in lengths, making 8 pieces
1 tablespoon honey	
Skin from the chicken	½ green pepper, seeded and diced, making 8 pieces
	8 bamboo or metal skewers

1 To make the sauce, put the soy sauce, *mirin*, sugar, honey, and chicken skin into a saucepan, bring to a boil, and simmer for about 10 minutes or until thickened.

2 To prepare the *yakitori*, thread onto a skewer pieces of chicken, leek, chicken, green pepper, and chicken again, in that order.

3 Heat the broiler to low and cook the *yakitori* until the meat has turned white (about 3 minutes).

4 Turn up the heat to medium and brush the *yakitori* with the sauce frequently, turning from time to time, for about 6–7 minutes or until the meat is cooked through. Serve with rice and a vegetable dish.

CHICKEN LIVERS with Peppers in a Sweet Soy Sauce

REBA TO PIMAN NO AMAKARA-NI

Chicken livers are widely eaten in Japan. Cooking in soy sauce and sugar disguises the smell of the liver, which some people dislike, and softens the flesh.

INGREDIENTS

¼ lb chicken livers, cut into bite-sized pieces

1 tablespoon vegetable oil

½ green pepper, seeded and thinly sliced lengthwise

1½ tablespoons soy sauce

1½ tablespoons mirin

½ tablespoon sugar

1 Dip the livers into a bowl of boiling water until blanched, then drain.

2 Heat the oil in a skillet and saute the green pepper for about 3 minutes. Remove and set aside.

3 Add the livers to the pan, frying over a medium heat for about 7 minutes. Sprinkle on the soy sauce, *mirin,* and sugar and continue to cook, stirring, for about 5 minutes.

4 Return the green pepper to the skillet and stir in lightly for a few minutes. Serve hot with rice and a vegetable dish.

DEEP-FRIED CHICKEN Nuggets

TORI NO KARA-AGE

The mixture of garlic, ginger, and soy sauce enhances the taste of the chicken, with the sliced lemon giving a refreshing "bite" to these delicious nuggets.

INGREDIENTS

2 boneless chicken breasts, cut into bite-sized cubes

FOR THE MARINADE

3 tablespoons soy sauce

1 oz gingerroot, peeled and grated

2 large garlic cloves, peeled and grated

Salt and freshly ground black pepper

FOR THE COATING

2 tablespoons cornstarch

2 tablespoons all-purpose flour

Vegetable oil, for deep frying

2 slices lemon, to garnish

1 Marinate the chicken with the soy sauce, ginger, garlic, salt and pepper for 30 minutes.

2 Mix the cornstarch with the all-purpose flour. Take each piece of chicken from the marinade and roll in the flour mixture until completely coated.

3 Heat the oil to 350°F and deep-fry the chicken pieces for 4–5 minutes or until a burnished golden brown. Garnish with the sliced lemon and serve on a bed of salad leaves.

TOFU HAMBURGER

TOFU HAMBURGER

A modern, healthy Japanese variation of an all-American favorite. The *tofu* should be *momen* (coarser, solid *tofu*) which needs to be left to drain for a few minutes before it is used so that it is not too watery.

MAKES 4 BURGERS

¼ cup chopped carrot
2 scallions, chopped
1 cup ground chicken
7 oz momen, or "cotton" tofu
½ egg, beaten
1 tablespoon fresh bread crumbs
1 tablespoon all-purpose flour
Salt and freshly ground black pepper
1 tablespoon vegetable oil
2 slices lemon, to garnish
Soy sauce, to serve

1 Grate the carrot and scallions in a food processor. Add the chicken, tofu, egg, bread crumbs, flour, salt and pepper, and continue to process until well mixed.

2 Divide the mixture into 4 equal portions and form into burger shapes.

3 Heat the oil in a skillet and cook the burgers over low heat for about 8 minutes on each side or until browned. Serve with soy sauce and garnish with lemon slices.

FRIED MARINATED Herrings

NISHIN NO TSUKE-YAKI

This is an easy-to-prepare and quick meal. Marinating the herrings in *sake* and soy sauce adds extra flavor.

INGREDIENTS

2 large or 4 small herrings, gutted and boned

2 tablespoons all-purpose flour

2 tablespoons vegetable oil

FOR THE MARINADE	FOR THE DRESSING
4 teaspoons sake	4 teaspoons soy sauce
4 teaspoons soy sauce	2 teaspoons wine vinegar
	1 teaspoon sugar

1 Mix together the *sake* and soy sauce, then pour it over the herrings and marinate for 30 minutes, turning 2 or 3 times.

2 Meanwhile, make the dressing by mixing the soy sauce, vinegar, and sugar in a bowl.

3 Wipe the herrings with paper towels and then coat with the flour.

4 Heat the vegetable oil in a skillet and saute the herrings for about 3 minutes on each side or until the flour coating is golden brown. Serve with rice and a vegetable dish.

DEEP-FRIED MACKEREL

SABA NO TASUTA-AGE

T he venerable mackerel is one of the mainstays of the Japanese diet and can be prepared in numerous ways. *Age-mono*, or deep-frying, locks in the mackerel's oils, which gives its flesh a meat-like quality.

INGREDIENTS

1 x 1 lb mackerel, head removed and gutted
1 tablespoon soy sauce
½ tablespoon sake
½ fresh chili, seeded and finely chopped
½ in cube gingerroot, crushed
2–3 tablespoons cornstarch
Vegetable oil, for deep frying

1 Cut the mackerel in half, slicing close to one side of the backbone. Repeat the same process on the other side. Now you have 2 filets separated from the backbone. Remove as many bones from the filets as possible without spoiling the flesh (a pair of tweezers is helpful). Cut each filet into three pieces.

2 Put the soy sauce, *sake*, chili pepper, and ginger into a dish and marinate the fish for 20

3 Dry the fish using paper towels to remove any excess moisture, then coat in the cornstarch. Heat the oil to 350°F, then deep-fry the fish for about 4 minutes. Serve with stir-fried vegetables and sprinkle with soy sauce.

BROILED SALTED TROUT

MASU NO SHIO-YAKI

Broiling is a very simple way of cooking fish. The trout need to be fresh to make the most of this dish.

INGREDIENTS

2 medium trout, gutted

1 teaspoon salt

Soy sauce, to serve

① Make 3 cuts on each side of the fish, place them on a wire rack, and sprinkle both sides with salt.

② Broil for 5–6 minutes or until lightly browned, then turn and broil for a further 5–6 minutes. (Remember the cooking time will vary depending on the size of the fish). When the fish is ready, transfer to a plate and sprinkle with soy sauce. Serve with rice and a vegetable dish.

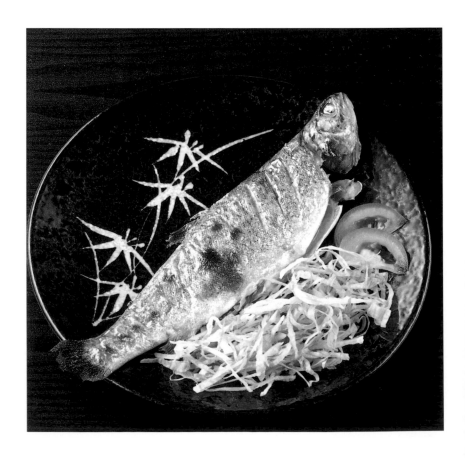

SIMMERED MACKEREL *in Miso Sauce*

SABA NO MISO-NI

This dish is a particular favorite in the fall, when the *saba* (mackerel) is reputed to be at its best. The *saba* is cooked with the bones to give extra flavor.

INGREDIENTS

1 x 1 lb mackerel, head removed
and gutted

FOR THE SAUCE

½ cup water

2 tablespoons sugar

1 tablespoon sake

2 oz miso

1 thin slice peeled gingerroot

2 scallions, cut in half

1 Cut the mackerel in half close to one side of the backbone to make 2 pieces of fish, one with the backbone attached and one without. Cut each piece in half again.

2 Put the water, sugar, sake, and miso in a pan, then heat until the liquid is simmering. Add the fish and ginger and continue to simmer for 7–8 minutes, covered with a lid slightly smaller than the pan and placed directly over the fish. Use aluminum foil if you do not have a lid the right size.

3 Add the scallions and simmer for a further 5–10 minutes. Serve immediately with rice and a vegetable dish.

SIMMERED SQUID with Mouli

DAIKON TO IKA NO UMA-NI

The flavor of this dish comes from the subtle taste of the squid combined with the fresh mouli. Mouli, the Italian giant radish, is easier to cook than Japanese daikon, because of its higher water content.

INGREDIENTS

1 x ¼ lb squid
¼ lb mouli, peeled, cut in half lengthwise and cut into ½ in pieces
¼ cup sake
¼ cup soy sauce
½ cup water

1 Pull the head and tentacles from the squid, then remove the transparent center bone and wash the body cavity. Take off the skin, then cut the head from the tentacles.

2 Cut the body and legs of the squid into ½-inch widths and blanch in boiling water. Put the mouli in a pan and cover with cold water. Bring to a boil and simmer for about 6 minutes until the mouli has become almost transparent, then drain.

3 Heat the *sake* in a pan with the soy sauce. When it boils, add the squid and simmer for about 4 minutes. Remove the squid with a slotted spoon and set aside.

4 Add the water and drained mouli to the pan, simmer, covered, for about 7 minutes. Put the squid in the pan with the mouli and simmer for 3–4 minutes. Serve with rice and a vegetable dish.

FRIED EGGPLANT and Green Pepper in Sweet *Miso* Sauce

NASU NO NABE-SHIGI

Autumn is the season for eggplants in Japan, when grocers stock their shelves with the numerous varieties available. Japanese eggplants vary greatly in length, though none possess the girth of those typically produced in the United States.

INGREDIENTS

2 tablespoons sesame oil
1 medium onion, peeled and cut into bite-sized pieces
1 x ½ lb eggplants, cut into bite-sized pieces and soaked in water
½ green pepper, cut into bite-sized pieces

FOR THE SWEET *MISO* SAUCE

1½ oz miso paste
2 tablespoons sugar
2 tablespoons water
2 tablespoons mirin

1 Heat 1 tablespoon of sesame oil in a pan and saute the onion for 3–4 minutes. Add the rest of the oil and the eggplant and continue to fry for 3–4 minutes. Add the green pepper and fry until the eggplant has softened.

2 Mix together the *miso* paste, sugar, water, and *mirin* in a bowl, then add to the pan, stirring for 1–2 minutes. Serve hot as a side dish.

SPINACH with *Bonito Flakes and Soy Sauce*

HOURENSO NO O-HITASHI

Fresh spinach is vital to make this delicious, nutritious dish. Take care not to overcook the spinach or you will destroy its vitamins.

INGREDIENTS

⅓ lb spinach leaves, rinsed and drained
A pinch of salt
A large pinch of bonito fish flakes
2–3 tablespoons soy sauce

1 Boil the spinach in salted water for about 2 minutes or until lightly cooked.

2 Drain and quickly rinse with cold water to cool and avoid discoloration.

3 Holding the leaves in a bunch at the stem, squeeze out any excess water.

4 Cut the bunch into 1-inch lengths. Place in a small bowl or dish and sprinkle with the bonito flakes, followed by a drizzle of soy sauce. Serve as a side dish.

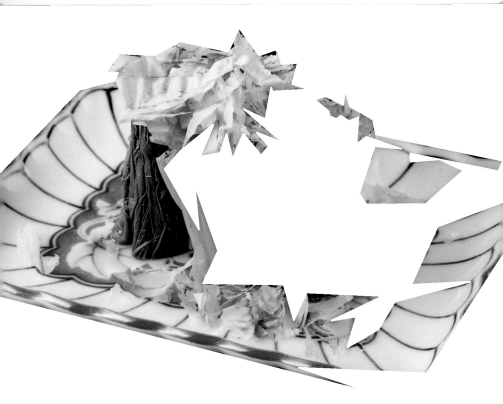

BRAISED SWEET POTATOES

SATSUMA-IMO NO AMA-NI

A traditional favorite, sweet potatoes are eaten throughout the year in Japan. This simple dish brings out their delicate sweetness.

INGREDIENTS

¼ lb sweet potatoes, cut into ½ in pieces
⅓ cup water
A pinch of salt
1 tablespoon sugar
1 teaspoon soy sauce

1 With a knife, bevel off the edges of the sweet potato. This will help prevent them from breaking up during cooking.

2 Put the potatoes, water, salt, sugar, and soy sauce into a large pan, making sure that the pieces of potato are laid flat on the bottom. Bring to a boil, then simmer, covered, for 10–15 minutes, until the potatoes have softened, removing the lid for the last 5 minutes. (Remember that the simmering time required will depend on the type of sweet potatoes you use.) Serve as a side dish.

SIMMERED CABBAGE and Bacon

CABETSU TO BECON NO NI-BITASHI

Japanese cabbage has a softer texture than those available in the U.S. Accordingly, I think it is best to discard, or use for another recipe, the tougher, outer leaves of the cabbage and use only the inner leaves for this dish. Try not to overcook the cabbage, or it will become limp. The leaves should be cooked, but should still have some crunch left in them.

INGREDIENTS

½ lb cabbage leaves, cut into 1 in squares

2 slices of bacon, cut into 1 in lengths

1¼ cups dashi stock (see p. 13)

2 teaspoons soy sauce

2 teaspoons vegetable oil

1 Heat the oil in a pan and fry the bacon over a low heat until cooked.

2 Add the cabbage and saute, stirring, for 2 minutes.

3 Add the *dashi* stock and soy sauce. Simmer, covered for 10 minutes, or until the cabbage has softened. Stir occasionally. Serve as a side dish.

STIR-FRIED SNOW PEAS and Luncheon M

SAYA-INGEN TO CORNBEEF NO ITAME-MONO

It has been said many times that the Japanese are a nation of innovators, and this dish illustrates the Japanese habit of absorbing a foreign influence into their culture and then enhancing it with a distinctive Japanese flavor. The snow peas should be firm, so be careful not to overcook them.

INGREDIENTS

1 cup snow peas, rinsed and trimmed
1 tablespoon vegetable oil
¼ lb luncheon meat, chopped
1 teaspoon soy sauce
Salt and freshly ground black pepper

❶ Boil the snow peas in salted water for 3 minutes, then drain.

❷ Heat the oil in a skillet. Add the luncheon meat and stir-fry for 5 minutes over a medium heat.

❸ Add the snow peas, sprinkle with salt and pepper, and stir-fry for another 5 minutes. Sprinkle with the soy sauce. Serve hot as a side dish.

CHINESE LEAVES and Clams in Mustard and Soy Sauce

HAKUSAI TO TORI-GAI NO KARASHI-JOYU AE

Clams are the traditional ingredient used for this dish, but other small shellfish can be used to make an excellent and economical substitute. You can use fresh clams or those sold in jars or cans.

INGREDIENTS

¼ lb Chinese cabbage
4 scallions
½ tablespoon soy sauce
1 teaspoon English mustard
1 teaspoon mirin
¼ lb baby clams, drained

1 Bring a saucepan of water to a boil, add the Chinese cabbage and cook for 3 minutes. Then, add the scallions and boil for a further 2 minutes. Drain and rinse lightly with cold water, then squeeze out any excess water. Cut into 1-inch lengths.

2 Mix the soy sauce, mustard, and *mirin* in a large bowl. Add the Chinese cabbage, scallions, and clams and mix. Serve as a side dish or as an appetizer.

GREEN BEANS in a Sesame Dressing

INGEN NO GOMA-AE

Sesame enjoys a reputation of being a healthy food in Japan, and both black and white sesame seeds are common ingredients in Japanese cuisine. To toast the seeds for this recipe, simply put them in a skillet without oil, then heat while stirring until the seeds have puffed up and you can smell the distinctive aroma of sesame.

INGREDIENTS

½ lb frozen whole green beans

A pinch of salt

FOR THE DRESSING

1 tablespoon toasted sesame seeds

1 tablespoon sugar

⅔ tablespoon dashi stock (see p. 13)

½ tablespoon miso paste

1 tablespoon soy sauce

1 Boil the beans in a pan of boiling water for 5 minutes or until tender.

2 Finely grind the sesame seeds in a pestle and mortar or in a coffee grinder. Add the sugar, *dashi*, *miso* paste, and soy sauce and mix together well.

3 Toss the green beans in the sesame dressing and serve as a side dish.

SIMMERED Mixed Vegetables

YASAI NO NI-MONO

The potato is not a staple part of the Japanese diet, but is nevertheless much used in Japanese cooking. It is usually diced and cooked with other vegetables as in this dish.

INGREDIENTS

¾ cup dashi stock (see p. 13)

¼ lb carrots, peeled and chopped at random into bite-sized pieces

½ lb potatoes, peeled and cut into bite-sized pieces

1 medium onion, sliced

2 teaspoons sugar

½ tablespoon mirin

A pinch of salt

1 tablespoon soy sauce

¼ lb frozen whole green beans, halved

1 Put the *dashi*, carrots, and potatoes in a pan. Bring to a boil and simmer, covered, for 5 minutes.

2 Add the onion, sugar, *mirin*, salt, and soy sauce and continue to simmer, covered, for a further 5 minutes.

3 Finally, add the beans and simmer as before for 4 minutes. Serve hot as a side dish.

SEAFOOD SALAD with *Ponzu* Dressing

KANI KAMOBOKO IRI SALADA

*P*onzu can be used as a dip sauce (see Cod and Chinese Cabbage Pot on page 72) or as a tangy, non-oily salad dressing. It is equally good used in both ways.

INGREDIENTS

2 celery sticks
3 in piece cucumber
¼ lb carrots, peeled
⅛ lb frozen whole green beans
5 seafood sticks
A pinch of salt
1 quantity of ponzu dressing (see p. 72)

❶ Slice the celery, cucumber, and carrot on a slant, then cut into matchsticks (see p.9 for more information).

❷ Cook the green beans in salted boiling water for 4–5 minutes, then rinse with cold water, drain, and cut in half.

❸ Mix the vegetables together on a plate or in a bowl. Then pull the seafood sticks into strands with your fingers and use to garnish the top of the salad. Drizzle with the *ponzu* dressing to serve.

TEMPURA

TEMPURA

One of the most famous dishes in the Japanese repertoire, *Tempura* needs no introduction. Ironically, strong evidence exists that *Tempura* is not originally Japanese but was introduced into Japan by Portuguese traders in the seventeenth century. One of the great advantages of *Tempura* is its versatility. Virtually any seafood and vegetable can be prepared and served in this way. The ingredients suggested below are those most commonly served in Japan. Mix the dip first, so that the *Tempura* can be served and eaten immediately after being fried.

INGREDIENTS

½ *green pepper, seeded and cut into four pieces lengthways*

4 shiitake mushrooms

175 g (6 oz) sweet potatoes, unpeeled but sliced into 7 mm (¼ in) rounds

100 g (4 oz) carrots, peeled and cut into 6 cm (2½ in) lengths, then cut into matchsticks

4 king prawns, peeled but tails on

Vegetable oil, for deep frying

A little plain flour

1 small mouli, peeled and grated

FOR THE BATTER

75 g (3 oz) plain flour

25 g (1 oz) cornflour

1 egg, beaten

150 ml (5 fl oz) water

FOR THE DIP

2 tablespoons mirin

2 tablespoons soy sauce

150 ml (5 fl oz) dashi stock (see p.13)

❶ To make the dip, put the *mirin*, soy sauce and *dashi* stock in a pan, bring to the boil and simmer for 1 minute. Leave to cool.

❷ To make the batter, place the flour, cornflour, egg and water into a bowl and mix lightly using chopsticks or a fork. The batter should be quite lumpy with some flour visible on top of the mixture.

❸ Heat the oil in a pan to 180°C/350°F. Check the temperature by dropping in some batter or a piece of bread, if it bubbles and floats to the surface, the oil is at the right temperature.

5 Dip the vegetables into the batter and deep fry until the batter has turned a golden brown. Check the harder vegetables, such as sweet potatoes, are cooked by piercing with a skewer. If it runs through smoothly with no resistance, the vegetables are ready. The carrot matchsticks should be picked up in small bunches, dipped in the batter and then fried, held together by the batter.

4 To deep fry the prawns, coat them with a little flour before dipping into the batter as this will stop them from spitting while frying. When all the ingredients have been fried, serve immediately. Place the dip into small bowls and into the centre, add a dessertspoonful of grated mouli. Dip the pieces of *Tempura* into the dip before eating. The dip and grated mouli should be replenished throughout the meal.

JAPANESE-STYLE OMELETTE

TAMAGO-YAKI

Often served for breakfast in Japan, *tamago-yaki* requires a little more skill and patience than a Western omelet, but the delicious result is well worth the extra effort. It is essential to use a non-stick skillet to get a really good result.

INGREDIENTS

2 eggs
½ tablespoon sugar
½ tablespoon soy sauce
½ tablespoon dashi stock (see p.13)
A pinch of salt
Vegetable oil, for frying

1 Break the eggs into a bowl, add the sugar, soy sauce, *dashi* stock, and salt and mix well. Heat the oil in a non-stick skillet over a low heat. Pour one quarter of the egg mixture into the skillet.

2 Just before the surface of the egg starts to get firm, carefully flip over the edge and roll up. Store on one side of the pan.

3 Holding up the rolled omelet with a spatula or chopstick, add a second quarter of the egg mixture, making sure that it spreads beneath the already cooked roll.

4 Again, just before the egg begins to firm, roll around the completed roll and store on the other side of the pan. Repeat this process with the two remaining quarters of egg mixture. Cool before cutting into 1-inch lengths. When served as a side dish, sprinkle with soy sauce.

SEAWEED-WRAPPED Avocado

AVOCADO TO NORI

Avocado is not a traditional ingredient of Japanese cooking, but it is certainly popular in many Japanese homes. This popularity is said to be due to the similarity between the taste of the avocado and the taste of raw tuna as used in *sushi* and *sashimi*. You can mix in *wasabi*, the green Japanese mustard powder, to spice up the soy sauce, which can be used as a dressing, if you wish.

INGREDIENTS

1 avocado
Nori (*2 sheets of dried seaweed*)
2 teaspoons soy sauce
1 teaspoon wasabi (*optional*)

1 Slice the avocado in two, remove the pit, and peel. Cut in half again, then slice into ½-inch widths.

2 Cut the nori into strips and wrap the avocado slices in the *nori*.

3 Pour soy sauce into a small dish. If you are using *wasabi*, mash in a small amount. Dip the avocado into the sauce before eating.

SALTED CABBAGE and Cucumber

CABETSU TO KYUURI NO SHIO-MOMI

This quickly-prepared side dish makes a superb partner to fresh cooked white rice. A sharp knife will help you cut the cucumber.

INGREDIENTS

¼ lb green cabbage (preferably the softer, inner leaves)
1½ in chunk cucumber, halved lengthwise
1 teaspoon salt
1 small red chili pepper, seeded and finely chopped

1 Cut the stalks out of the cabbage leaves, then slice the leaves lengthwise, before cutting into ½-inch widths. Slice the two halves of the cucumber as finely as you can.

2 Put the cabbage and cucumber in a bowl and sprinkle with the salt. Leave for 30 minutes, then squeeze out any excess liquid from the vegetables with your hands.

3 Add the chili pepper and mix well. Leave for 5 minutes.

4 Sprinkle with soy sauce just before serving.

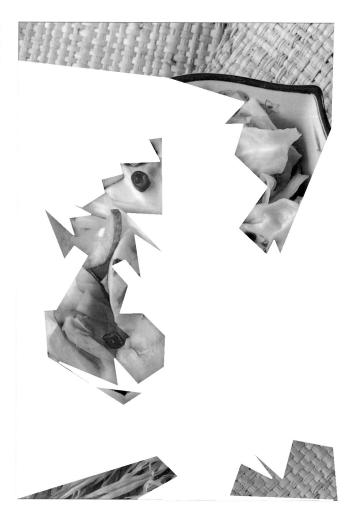

SALTED TURNIP with Lemon

KABU NO SOKUSEKI-ZUKE

This dish is one of many Japanese *tsukemono* or pickles.
The freshness of the turnip is essential for success.

INGREDIENTS

½ lb turnips peeled, halved,
and thinly sliced

1 teaspoon salt

3 lemon slices, cut into quarters

1 teaspoon soy sauce

1 Place the sliced turnip in a bowl, sprinkle with the salt, and leave for 20–30 minutes.

2 Rub the turnip until it is soft, then squeeze out any excess liquid.

3 Add the lemon quarters, then drizzle with soy sauce. Serve as a side dish.

SIMMERED *HIJIKI* SEAWEED

HIJIKI NO NI-MONO

H ijiki is one of the many types of seaweed used in
Japanese cooking. *Hijiki* is a very healthy source
of several minerals, including calcium and iodine and
vitamin B^{12}.

INGREDIENTS

¼ oz dried hijiki
½ sheet abura-age
¼ lb carrots, peeled, and cut into short matchsticks
2 teaspoons vegetable oil
1 cup dashi stock (see p.13)
1½ tablespoons sugar
1½ tablespoons soy sauce
1 tablespoon mirin

1 Rinse the *hijiki*, then soak in a bowl of water for 20–30 minutes. Rinse, then drain again. The *hijiki* should swell to six or seven times its original size.

2 Rinse the *abura-age* with hot water, then cut into small slices, about the same size as the carrot.

3 Heat the oil in a saucepan and saute the *hijiki*, *abura-age*, and carrots for 1 minute.

4 Add the *dashi* stock, sugar, soy sauce, and *mirin*, then simmer, uncovered, for about 25 minutes or until the liquid has almost evaporated. Serve as a side dish. Any leftovers can be kept refrigerated for 3–4 days.

BRAISED SOYBEANS

DAIZU NO AMA-NI

The humble soybean is the most widely used ingredient in Japanese cuisine, forming the basis for soy sauce, *tofu,* and *miso.* Soybeans are rich in nutrients and fiber, and are regarded in Japan as "meat from the earth."

INGREDIENTS

3 dried shiitake mushrooms
3 in dried kelp, wiped with a damp cloth
1 lb can soybeans, drained
⅛ lb carrots, peeled and diced
2 tablespoons sugar
1½ tablespoons soy sauce

1 Soak the shiitake mushrooms and kelp in ⅞ cup of water for 30 minutes. Reserve the water. Dice the shiitake mushrooms and kelp into small pieces.

2 Put the kelp, mushrooms, and reserved water into a pan. Add the soybeans, carrot, an extra ½ cup of fresh water, and the sugar. Bring to a boil and cook, uncovered, for 15 minutes.

3 Add the soy sauce and simmer for a further 10 minutes. Serve as a side dish. Any leftovers can be stored in the refrigerator for up to a week.

CUCUMBER AND *WAKAME*

KYUURI TO WAKAME NO SANBAI-ZU

Although this is a cold dish, it is not regarded as a salad in Japan. If you can't get hold of rice vinegar, malt vinegar will do as a substitute.

INGREDIENTS

½ lb cucumber, cut in half lengthwise
and then sliced very thinly

1 teaspoon salt

½ tablespoon dried wakame soaked in hot
water for a few minutes until swollen

FOR THE SWEET AND SOUR DRESSING

5 teaspoons rice vinegar

½ tablespoon sugar

½ teaspoon soy sauce

❶ Put the cucumber in a bowl, sprinkle with the salt, and leave for 15 minutes.

❷ Taking the cucumber in your hands, squeeze out as much liquid as you can. Do the same with the *wakame*.

❸ Mix together the sugar, vinegar, and soy sauce in a small bowl.

❹ Just before eating, mix the dressing together with the cucumber and *wakame*. Serve as a side dish.

BASIC *SUSHI* RICE

SUSHI YO GOHAN

This is the basic technique for producing the glutinous, vinegar-flavored rice that forms the basis of all the variants of *sushi*. Japanese short-grain rice is essential for making sushi rice. The ratio of Japanese rice to water should be 1 part rice to 1¼ parts water.

INGREDIENTS

¼ cup Japanese short-grain rice
1 in strip dried kelp
1 cup water

FOR THE SUSHI-ZU

1½ tablespoons rice vinegar
1 tablespoon sugar
½ teaspoon salt

1 Put the rice in a pan and rinse several times until the water is almost clear. Leave the rice in a strainer for 30 minutes so the individual grains can begin to absorb the water remaining in the strainer. Add the water, rice, and kelp to a pan. Bring to a boil, taking the kelp out just before boiling point. Simmer, covered, for about 10 minutes. (Simmering time depends on the amount of rice you cook.)

2 Test the rice to see if it has softened. Turn off the heat and leave for 10 minutes. Mix the vinegar, sugar, and salt in a bowl. Put the rice in a large bowl. Wet the wooden spoon and add the *sushi-zu* a little at a time, "cutting" it into the rice with the wooden spoon (not stirring or mashing), until you have used all the liquid. The rice will now be giving off the sharp aroma of the *sushi-zu*. Set aside to cool before using.

"ROLL YOUR OWN" SUSHI

TEMAKI-ZUSHI

A modern and very popular variant on the *sushi* theme. *Temaki-zushi* makes a great change for dinner parties.

INGREDIENTS	FOR THE FILLING
1 quantity basic sushi rice (see p. 60)	*1 x 3½ oz can tuna in brine*
5 sheets of nori, each cut into 4 pieces	*1 tablespoon mayonnaise*
5 diagonal slices of cucumber, cut into long matchsticks	**FOR THE OMELETTE**
¼ avocado, sliced	*1 egg*
1 rollmop herring, sliced	*1 teaspoon sugar*
1 bunch cress	*A pinch of salt*
Soy sauce	*2 teaspoons vegetable oil, for frying*

❶ To prepare the filling, first drain the tuna and then mix with the mayonnaise. Make a Japanese style omelet (see p.52), which should be cut into strips after cooling down. Now lay all the ingredients out on a large serving plate. The rice is laid out on a separate plate, as are the strips of *nori*.

❷ Each diner takes a piece of *nori* in one hand and scoops about a tablespoon of rice onto it, spreading it quite thinly.

❸ Next, a portion of one or a combination of the fillings are taken with *hashi* and laid in the center of the sheet. Last, the diner rolls the *nori* into a cone shape, dipping it into his or her small bowl of soy sauce before eating.

THIN ROLLS of Cucumber and Pickled Radish

HOSO-MAKI ZUSHI: KAPPA-MAKI AND TAKUWAN-MAKI

Kappa-maki, or cucumber roll, is made with narrow strips of the cucumber. *Takuwan*, made by a process of drying, then pickling, the Japanese giant radish or *daikon*, is used for *takuwan-maki*. These two *hoso-maki* could be called "family sushi," as they are often made at home rather than being bought.

INGREDIENTS

1 quantity basic sushi *rice (see p. 60)*
2.5 sheets nori, *cut into half*
1 cucumber
2 takuwan *sticks of ¼ x 7½ in*
2½ teaspoons toasted sesame seeds
A little wasabi *(optional)*

❶ Cut the cucumber into 3 sticks each measuring ¼ x 7½ inches.

❷ Place the *nori* on a *sushi* mat or a chopping board covered with plastic wrap. Spread the rice evenly on the nori, except for a ¾-inch strip clear along the far edge. Using the tip of your finger, smooth a small amount of *wasabi* paste over the rice.

❸ Place a cucumber stick on the rice and sprinkle ½ teaspoon of toasted sesame seeds onto it.

❹ Roll over the *sushi* mat and form into shape. The *nori* is sealed by the moisture from the rice. In the same way, make 2 more *hoso-maki* with the cucumbers and make 2 with *takuwan*. Cut each roll into 5 pieces using a knife dipped in a mixture of water and vinegar to give a clean cut.

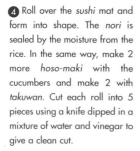

**HOW TO CUT THE CUCUMBER
AND *TAKUWAN***

*With a sharp knife, pare a ½-inch thick strip
from the length of the cucumber. Next, slice
down each side of the center of the strip
lengthwise, so that you have three strips of
roughly equal size. Prepare the takuwan in
the same way.*

LARGE *SUSHI* ROLLS

FUTO-MAKI ZUSHI

Y ou might think it takes real skill and experience to produce good *futo-maki*, but after a couple of practice runs, you should get the hang of it. Nevertheless, well-made *futo-maki* will undoubtedly impress your dinner guests.

INGREDIENTS

1 quantity basic sushi *rice (see p. 60)*
3 dried shiitake mushrooms, rinsed and soaked in ¼ cup water
1 teaspoon sugar
1 tsp soy sauce
2 sheets nori *seaweed sheets*
6 seafood sticks
1 bunch watercress

FOR THE OMELETTE

1 egg, beaten
1 teaspoon sugar
A pinch of salt
Vegetable oil, for frying

1 To prepare the filling, slice the mushrooms and put them in a pan with the water they were soaked in, the sugar, and the soy sauce. Bring this mixture to a boil and simmer for 5 minutes. Put the sugar and salt into a bowl with the beaten egg and mix together well. Heat the oil in an omelet pan and make a Japanese-style omelet (see p.52). Let the omelet cool and then cut lengthwise into three strips.

2 Place the *nori* squarely on a *sushi* mat or a chopping board covered with plastic wrap. Spread the rice onto the *nori*, leaving a 1-inch strip free of rice at the far edge.

3 Next, lay, in order, half the omelet, shiitake, seafood sticks, and watercress in lines across the bed of rice, leaving a small strip of bare rice between each ingredient.

4 Now, holding the egg in place, pull the near edge of the *nori* sheet up and over in one motion until the *nori* has enfolded all the ingredients laid on the rice. Next, use your fingers to tuck the near edge of the *nori* inside the roll. Then, rotate the mat until the seam is turned to the bottom of the roll.

5 Grip the far end of the *sushi* mat with your right hand and hold the roll with your left. Now, pull the roll firmly toward you to make sure that the *futo-maki* becomes well packed. Finally, line up the sides of the mat by gently patting with the palms of your hands to clean up the ends of the roll. Gently unroll the mat to reveal the finished *futomaki* inside.

Repeat with the remaining half of the ingredients. When finished, slice the rolls into pieces the thickness of your thumb. Use a knife dipped in water mixed with vinegar so that the rice will not cling to the blade. Serve displayed on a large plate. The *futo-maki* should be taken from the plate and dipped into individual dishes of soy sauce before being eaten.

SALMON ROE *SUSHI*

IKURA-ZUSHI

Salmon roe is an expensive but popular ingredient in Japan. This dish makes a rather nice appetizer, although you can eat *Ikura-zushi* combined with rolled *sushi* or *Inari-zushi* as a main dish.

INGREDIENTS

4 tablespoons cooked sushi rice, see p.60
1½ x 5 in strips nori
2 slices cucumber, cut in half
4 teaspoons salmon roe

1 Wet your palm with a little water. Take 1 tablespoon of rice and form into a square-shaped ball. Make 3 other balls in the same way.

2 Place each rice ball in the middle of a strip of *nori*. Roll the *nori* around it, then stand it on a plate.

3 Place the sliced cucumber on top of each of the rice balls, and put 1 teaspoon of salmon roe on top of the cucumber. Serve with a dash of soy sauce.

FRIED BEAN-CURD *SUSHI*

INARI-ZUSHI

These sweet-tasting sacks of *sushi* rice can be eaten along with other *sushi* dishes or alone as a tasty and filling snack. *Inari-zushi* also forms a part of many a Japanese picnic, as well as being a firm favorite as a brown-bag filler. Refer to the instructions for making basic *sushi* rice while cooking the rice.

INGREDIENTS

½ quantity of basic sushi rice (see p. 60)
2 sheets abura-age (thin bean curd)
½ cup dashi stock (see p. 13)
1½ tablespoons sugar
1 tablespoon mirin
2 teaspoons soy sauce
1 teaspoon toasted sesame seeds

1 Gently roll the *abura-age*, using a chopstick as a rolling pin, to make it easier to handle. Place in a colander and rinse with hot water. Cut in half and gently open the "sack."

2 Put the *dashi* stock, *mirin*, soy sauce, and *abura-age* in a pan, bring to a boil, and simmer for 20 minutes or until the *dashi* mixture has almost evaporated. Make a small lid with some aluminum foil and place it on top of the *abura-age*. Continue to cook until the remaining liquid has been completely absorbed.

3 Remove the *abura-age* and leave on a plate or chopping board until dry.

4 Mix the *sushi* rice with the sesame and divide into 4 equal portions. Fill each *abura-age* with rice and fold to create a small sack.

JAPANESE RICE BALLS

ONIGIRI

*O*nigiri is a simply prepared and handy "eat anytime" meal that can be packed up in a picnic or served as an accompaniment at dinner. The use of the word "ball" is slightly misleading, as the shape of the finished product more closely resembles a triangle.

The use of Japanese rice for making rice balls is strongly recommended, as other varieties tend to lack the characteristic stickiness of the Japanese grains.

INGREDIENTS

¼ cup Japanese short-grain rice, rinsed well
A pinch of flaked bonito
¼ tablespoon soy sauce
1 Japanese pickled plum (ume-boshi), seeded and halved
4 strips 2 x 6 in nori

1 Rinse the rice until the water runs through almost clear.

2 Cook the rice the same way as for *sushi* rice (see p.60), but do not add the *sushi-zu*.

3 Let the rice cool down before use. Mix the *bonito* flakes with the soy sauce in a small saucer or plate to make a paste.

4 Wet and then sprinkle your palms with a little salt. (You will need to repeat this process with every ball you make.) Scoop up 3 heaped tablespoons of rice and mold it lightly into a round shape.

5 Once the rough ball shape is formed, make a small hole in the middle and put *either* half of the *bonito* paste or one half of the Japanese plum inside.

6 Cover the hole while at the same time trying to form the rice into a triangular shape.

7 When the 4 rice balls have been formed, wrap each with a strip of *nori*.

MIXED RICE

MAZE GOHAN

Japanese-style mixed rice is easy to make and can be served either as a main course with a soup and salad or instead of plain boiled rice to accompany other dishes.

INGREDIENTS

¼ cup Japanese short-grain rice	1 tablespoon sugar
⅛ lb carrot, peeled and cut into short matchsticks	1½ tablespoons soy sauce
	3 snow peas
3 shiitake mushrooms, cut into short matchsticks	A pinch of salt
½ sheet abura-age, rinsed in hot water and cut into short matchsticks	1 egg
	½ tablespoon water
¼ in piece koya dofu, soaked in water for 5 minutes, then cut into matchsticks	Vegetable oil, for frying
½ cup dashi stock (see p.13)	2 red radishes, thinly sliced

1 First make *sushi* rice according to the instructions on p.60.

2 Put the carrots, shiitake, *abura-age, tofu, dashi* stock, sugar, and soy sauce in a pan. Bring to a boil and simmer for 15 minutes.

3 Meanwhile, boil the snow peas in salted water for 3 minutes, then remove and cut finely on a slant.

4 Mix the egg, water, and a pinch of salt together in a bowl. Heat the vegetable oil in an omelet pan and make 2 thin omelets. Let the omelets cool, then cut each one in half, then slice it into thin strips.

5 When Step 2 is complete, mix the ingredients with the *sushi* rice. Place the rice mixture on a large plate. Spread the egg, then the snow peas over the top, and decorate with the radish and strips of *nori*.

CHICKEN AND EGG on Rice

OYAKO-DON

In Japan this dish is known as "parent and child on rice." The method of preparation means that the chicken is still tender and succulent when served. Long-grain rice can be used in this dish.

INGREDIENTS

¼ cup short-grain rice
⅔ cup dashi stock (see p.13)
1 tablespoon sugar
1 tablespoon mirin
3 tablespoons soy sauce
2 boneless chicken breasts, diced
1 medium onion, sliced
1 egg, beaten
Watercress, for garnishing

1 Rinse and boil the rice according to the directions on the package.

2 Bring the *dashi* stock, sugar, *mirin,* and soy sauce to a boil in a skillet. Add the chicken and onion. Simmer for about 8 minutes or until the chicken is cooked.

3 Pour in the egg, letting it set on top of the chicken without stirring. When the egg has set, sprinkle on some watercress as a garnish. Serve the mixture on top of the serving of rice.

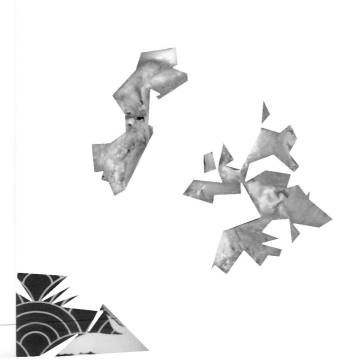

SUKIYAKI

SUKIYAKI

*S*ukiyaki is one of the few examples of Japanese cuisine to have become popular throughout the West. In Japan, a special, heavy pan is used, however *sukiyaki* can be prepared with any large, deep, frying pan. Like fondue, *sukiyaki* is always cooked at the table, with diners taking food from the pan as soon as it is ready. The pan is then replenished from a plate of fresh meat and vegetables standing by; therefore, there is no need for you to slave away over a hot stove!

INGREDIENTS

1 tablespoon vegetable oil	7 oz tofu, cut in half lengthwise and sliced
¼ cup dashi stock (see p13)	¼ lb Chinese cabbages, halved lengthwise and sliced
1½ tablespoons sugar	6 shiitake mushrooms, halved
2 tablespoons mirin	1 short leek, sliced on a slant
1 tablespoon sake	¼ lb beef, sliced paper thin
2½ tablespoons soy sauce	2 raw eggs (optional)
1 medium onion, halved and sliced	

❶ Heat the suet in a skillet and add the *dashi* stock, sugar, *mirin*, sake, and soy sauce. When this mixture begins to simmer, add half the amount of onions, *tofu*, Chinese cabbages, and shiitake, keeping each ingredient in its own separate group in the pan. Simmer for 7 minutes and then add half the beef, placing it in the center of the pan. Continue to simmer for several minutes until cooked.

❷ Break the raw eggs into 2 serving bowls and mix the yolk and white with your chopsticks. Take the cooked meat, *tofu,* and vegetables a few at a time from the pan, dip them into the raw egg, and eat with a bowl of rice. As the cooked ingredients are taken from the pan, re-plenish with the raw ingredients.

COD AND CHINESE Cabbage Pot

TARA TO HAKUSAI NO NABE

This very popular winter dish is normally cooked at the table using a portable burner. Everyone at the table takes food from the pan, transferring it to their own individual dishes, while the hostess keeps the pan stocked with fresh raw ingredients. You will need an 8-inch casserole dish.

INGREDIENTS

4 cups water
3 in piece dried konbu, or kelp
1 small leek, sliced on a slant into ½ in widths
1 medium onion, sliced
2 x ¼ lb cod filets or steaks, cut into large, bite-sized pieces
½ lb Chinese cabbage, cut in half lengthwise and then sliced into ½ in strips
¼ lb momen or "cotton" tofu, cut into ½ in cubes
¼ lb carrots, peeled and thinly sliced
4 shiitake mushrooms, cut into halves
6 snow peas

FOR THE PONZU DRESSING

3 tablespoons soy sauce
1 tablespoon lemon juice
1 tablespoon vinegar
1 tablespoon mirin
½ tablespoon Japanese instant stock granules

FOR THE GARNISH

1 x 1 lb mouli, peeled, grated, and lightly squeezed
A pinch of seven-spice or chili powder

1 Put the water and konbu in a heatproof casserole dish and bring to a boil. Add half the leek, onion, cod, Chinese cabbage, tofu, carrots, shiitake mushrooms, and snow peas, keeping groups together in the pan. Cook for 5–8 minutes, or until the vegetables are cooked.

2 Meanwhile, mix the soy sauce, lemon juice, vinegar, mirin, and dashi stock granules in a jar and stir well.

3 When roughly half of the cooked food has been taken from the casserole, replenish with the raw ingredients.

TO SERVE

Put 2 tablespoons of mouli and 1 tablespoon ponzu dressing into each serving bowl.

As you take food from the casserole with your chopsticks, dip it into the dressing and eat. Add some seven-spice if you wish to add a little more fire to the meal. As you eat, add more ponzu dressing and mouli when you need to. Serve with rice.

NOODLES in Soy Sauce Soup

SHOYU-RAMEN

*R*amen originally came from China, but has been adapted to suit Japanese tastes. It is universally popular as a lunch dish or light meal. Once you make the *ramen* stock, it can be kept in the refrigerator for a few days or can be frozen. Topping for *ramen* varies. Melted butter and corn are one of the most popular choices. *Ramen* noodles are sold both dried and fresh. Cooking times for the two types are much the same, but dried noodles do, of course, keep longer once purchased.

INGREDIENTS

FOR THE BASIC *RAMEN* STOCK
MAKES ABOUT 6 CUPS

A chicken carcass, roughly chopped
2 pork bones
½ leek
1 in piece gingerroot, peeled and cut in half
1 large garlic clove, cut in half
4 pints water

FOR THE *SHOYU RAMEN*

½ lb fresh ramen noodles
2½ cups ramen stock
3 tablespoons soy sauce
½ teaspoon salt
A pinch of freshly ground black pepper

FOR THE TOPPING

8 tablespoons corn kernels
3 scallions, chopped
4 teaspoons butter, cut in half

1 To make the *ramen* stock, blanch the chicken and pork bones. Then put the water, bones, leek, ginger, and garlic into a large pan. Bring to a boil and simmer for 1 hour, occasionally skimming off the scum. Strain the stock. Adjust the heat to prevent the stock from boiling again (which would make the liquid cloudy).

2 Boil the noodles for about 2–2½ minutes. Drain and put them in individual bowls.

3 Heat the 2½ cups of stock, soy sauce, salt, and pepper in a pan. When it boils, pour the soup into the bowls. Put 4 tablespoons of the corn on top of the noodles, sprinkle with the chopped scallion, then top with the butter. Eat as soon as possible or the noodles will absorb the soup and become soggy.

RAMEN NOODLES in Miso Soup

MISO RAMEN

R*amen* is Japanese fast-food. In this variation, the flavor of fried garlic and sesame oil complements the *miso* and chili. It is difficult not to make a noise when you eat Japanese noodles. In fact, the more you slurp, the better you will enjoy the meal, or so it is said!

INGREDIENTS	FOR THE TOPPING
½ lb fresh ramen *noodles*	1 tablespoon sesame oil
2½ cups ramen stock, (see p.74)	¼ lb bean sprouts
½ teaspoon salt	1 large garlic clove, sliced
A pinch of freshly ground black pepper	½ red sweet pepper, thinly sliced
2 teaspoons sesame oil	A pinch of chili powder
2 teaspoons toasted sesame seeds	A pinch of salt
3 tablespoons miso *paste*	

1 Cook the noodles for about 2–2½ minutes in boiling water. Drain and put into individual bowls.

2 Heat the stock and salt and pepper in a pan. When it boils, add the sesame oil and sesame seeds and stir in the *miso* paste until it has dissolved completely.

3 Meanwhile, heat the oil in a skillet. Stir-fry the bean sprouts, garlic, and red sweet pepper. Sprinkle in the pinch of chili pepper and salt. Place the vegetables on top of the noodles. Pour in the *miso* soup, serve and eat immediately.

BUCKWHEAT Noodles Topped with Deep-fried Giant Shrimp

TEMPURA SOBA

*S*oba noodles are made from buckwheat and are distinguished by their brown color. Like *ramen* noodles, they can be bought fresh or dried. *Soba* is considered to be a very healthy food by the Japanese, and topping a dish of the noodles with a giant shrimp turns a nourishing meal into a gourmet experience.

INGREDIENTS	FOR THE SOUP
2 giant shrimp	2½ cups dashi stock (see p.13)
A little all-purpose flour	1 teaspoon salt
4 shiitake mushrooms	2 teaspoons sugar
¼ lb dried soba	2 tablespoons mirin
FOR THE BATTER	2 tablespoons soy sauce
2 tablespoons all-purpose flour	2 scallions, chopped
½ egg, beaten	
4 tablespoons water	

1 To make the topping, mix the flour, egg, and water lightly in a bowl. Coat the shrimp with flour and dip in the batter. Dip the mushrooms into the batter. Heat the oil to 350°F and deep-fry until light golden brown.

2 Bring a large pan of water to a boil. Add the *soba* and cook for about 3 minutes. Briefly rinse with cold water and then drain. Divide the *soba* equally between two bowls.

3 Put the *dashi* stock, salt, sugar, *mirin*, and soy sauce in a pan and bring to a boil. Add to the bowls of *soba*.

4 Place one shrimp and two mushrooms on the top of each bowl and sprinkle with chopped scallion. Serve immediately.

WHEATFLOUR Noodles with Egg

KAKITAMA-UDON

*U*don is the name given by the Japanese to those noodles made from wheat flour. A great favorite in the winter months because of its warming properties, *udon* comes in various shapes, some flat, some round in section, some as thick as a little finger, others as thin as spaghetti.

INGREDIENTS

¼ lb fresh udon

FOR THE SOUP

2½ cups dashi stock *(see p. 13)*

1 teaspoon salt

2 teaspoons sugar

2 tablespoons mirin

2 tablespoons soy sauce

1 egg, beaten

2 teaspoons cornstarch

2 teaspoons water

2 scallions, chopped

1 Bring a large pan of water to a boil. Add the *udon* and boil for 2 minutes. Drain and place in equal portions in the 2 bowls.

2 Put the *dashi*, salt, sugar, *mirin*, and soy sauce in a pan and bring to a boil. Pour ⅔ of the liquid into the 2 bowls. Bring the remainder back to a boil and gradually add the egg, mixing lightly so that when the egg rises to the surface, it is cooked in fronds.

3 Mix the cornstarch and water into a paste and then add this to the soup to thicken. Pour the egg mixture into the bowls. Sprinkle with the scallion and serve immediately.

GLOSSARY

Abura-age Deep fried thin beancurd, usually sliced and used as a garnish or slit into a pocket and stuffed with rice. *Abura-age* can be frozen but does not keep longer than 48 hours refrigerated.

Dried shiitake The most common mushroom used in Japanese cookery, its taste and texture differs significantly from other types. If bought dried, soak in water for at least 30 minutes prior to use. The water can be reserved for later use in *dashi*.

Konbu *Konbu* or kelp is one of the best sources of iodine available and also contains several other important minerals. Care should be taken not to over-boil *konbu* as it very quickly becomes bitter. Wipe to prepare *konbu* for cooking but do not rinse, as this will wash away many of the nutrients.

Koya dofu Freeze-dried *tofu* which will keep for up to 6 months in its dried form. To prepare for use,

soak in water until the *tofu* has swollen and become spongy.

Mirin Japanese cooking wine, though with only a trace of alcohol. This syrupy rice derivative imparts a distinctive sweet flavour to the dishes in which it is used.

Miso This is made from fermenting cooked soya beans with a Japanese type of yeast known as *koji*. *Miso* is unique to Japanese cuisine and widely used both as a flavouring and as the basis for dressings. It is rich in protein. Kept refrigerated, it will last for several months. There are two common types: white *miso* (made from a rice-based yeast) and red *miso* (made from a barley yeast). White *miso* is more commonly used in soups while the red type finds favour as a general purpose flavouring and for dishes where a richer flavour is desired.

Nori The most widely used seaweed, sold in

paper-thin sheets. Before use, *nori* is toasted quickly under a grill or over a gas ring until the colour changes from an almost inky black to dark green. Some pre-toasted *nori* is available, so take care to check which sort you are buying.

Rice vinegar Known as *su*, Japanese rice vinegar is made from naturally fermented rice. Clear *su* is common and suitable for *sushi* rice. Brown *su*, which is the unrefined basis for white *su*, can be used in any recipe where the colour of the vinegar is not important to the final dish.

Sake Japanese rice wine, made all over Japan as well as in the United States. Unlike Western cooking, *sake* is only used sparingly in Japanese cookery. *Sake* is now widely available in the West, but if you cannot get it, you can use dry sherry instead.

Soy sauce Ubiquitous to Japanese cookery, this combination of fermented

GLOSSARY

soya beans, wheat and salt is a lighter, sweeter solution than Chinese soy. Japanese brands such as Kikkoman are now widely available.

Wakame A seaweed typically used in Japanese soups and salads. *Wakame* can be used after simply dipping into boiling water. *Wakame* should never be cooked for long. It can be bought dried, in which case soaking for 5 minutes in cold water will make it ready for any cooking application.

Wasabi Misleadingly translated as 'horseradish', *wasabi* is ground from the *Wasabia japanica*, a Japanese riverside plant. Like English mustard, *wasabi* can be bought ready made, or in powder form to be mixed with a little water. Powdered *wasabi* is better than the ready-made variety, which tends to lose its "bite" fairly quickly.

INDEX